DIRECTORY OF THE V

ESSENTIAL TRANSLATIONS SERIES 25

swiss arts council

pr helvetia

FABIANO ALBORGHETTI

DIRECTORY OF
THE VULNERABLE

Translated from the Italian
by Marco Sonzogni

AN ITALIAN-ENGLISH BILINGUAL EDITION

GUERNICA
TORONTO – BUFFALO – LANCASTER (U.K.)
2014

Michael Mirolla, editor
Guernica Editions Inc.
P.O. Box 76080, Abbey Market, Oakville (ON), Canada L6M 3H5
2250 Military Road, Tonawanda, N.Y. 14150-6000 U.S.A.
Distributors:
University of Toronto Press Distribution,
5201 Dufferin Street, Toronto (ON), Canada M3H 5T8
Gazelle Book Services, White Cross Mills, High Town, Lancaster LA1 4XS U.K.

First edition.
Typesetting by Antonio D'Alfonso
Printed in Canada.
Legal Deposit – First Quarter
Library of Congress Catalog Card Number: 2013950995
Library and Archives Canada Cataloguing in Publication
Alborghetti, Fabiano, 1970-, author
Directory of the vulnerable / Fabiano Alborghetti ;
translated from the Italian by Marco Sonzogni.
(Essential translations series ; 25)
Includes Registro dei fragili with English translation.
Poems.
Issued in print and electronic formats.
ISBN 978-1-55071-909-3 (pbk.).--ISBN 978-1-55071-910-9 (epub).--
ISBN 978-1-55071-911-6 (mobi)
I. Sonzogni, Marco, 1971-, translator II. Title.
III. Series: Essential translations series ; 25
PQ4901.L36R4313 2014   851'.92   C2013-906660-8
                                                   C2013-906661-6

CONTENTS

II
Judicial Theses
(Tesi del giudizio)

III
Directory of the Vulnerable
(Registro dei fragili)

PREFACE

Fabiano Alborghetti – a Milanese who has been living in Lugano for some time – sets out for us a vision of poetry directly opposite to much of the current poetic diction. Born in 1970, Alborghetti arrives at *Directory of the Vulnerable* (*Registro dei fragili*, 2009) after a rather complex process: a trail of small editions, publications in reviews and anthologies, a dedicated participation in the debates of the last decade, and, at the same time, a detached outlook, almost that of an outsider. Nevertheless, over the last few years readers and critics have noticed his search for words to describe expressive and external realities in areas of dire poverty. This appeared in the collection *The Opposite Bank* (*L'opposta riva*, 2006), in which Alborghetti energetically tried out his own idea of poetry – a sort of poetry-journalism anchored in the real world, as far from the effusion of lyricism as from playfulness as end to itself, but equally distant from a journalistic sociological realism. To write *The Opposite Bank,* the author spent years around the camp sites of illegal immigrants in the suburbs of Milan; he spent a good part of his spare time with them, sharing their experiences, as far as it was possible to share them, studying, taking notes, trying to understand. As a consequence, he tried to give a voice to those who had no voice, to those who seemed condemned to a shadowy existence, marginalised, denied. The result is a small but remarkable book which for many readers seemed to rival its great inspiration, Masters' *Spoon River,* but a more despairing *Spoon River,* edgy and set in our shattered present. Alborghetti was well aware of the risks he was facing with such a project: to fall into sentimentalism, into predictable denunciation or into politically correct cheap sentiments. Now, surprising his reader, he opted to write in a demanding and complex style, in which the experience of marginalisation and rootlessness resonate gradually by fragments, by shocking images: a mixture of atrociously realistic subject matter and a quite elevated poetic language, often cold and formal, producing surprising effects with an expressive vigour of which a single example will suffice:

Non aveva mai pregato in questo luogo
e il peso della solitudine sentiva maggiore
dall'arrivo e antecedente: sono morti

tutti prima che io arrivassi, al massimo ricordo
gli odori ma neanche i nomi adesso.
E qui o là diceva che terra vuoi che sia dove l'uomo

smette d'essere uomo e diventa animale, che Dio vede?

(He had never prayed in that place
and he felt the weight of solitude more heavily
since he came and what had happened; they had all died

before I came; at best I can recall
smells but no longer the names.
And he said, here or there, what country is it where a man

stops being human and becomes an animal, while God looks on?)

It is not easy to define the cultural origins of an author of this kind: one might think of Giovanni Giudici; of Elio Pagliarani (particularly, perhaps, his *La ragazza Carla*) or even of an unexpected elaboration of Giampiero Neri, by trying to link him with a different, experimental writing like that of Tiziano Rossi. But earlier points of reference include hypothetical precursors like Parini, Porta, and the ideas of Paolo Valera on the need to immerse oneself like a deep-sea diver in the reality of the world; there is a certain English influence, for example, Tony Harrison and his *V. and Other Poems;* or even more so, the synthetic and formal closure aimed at expressing a burning

8

socio-political reality in some of the more extreme examples of Durs Grünbein's work.

Starting from something like that, and from a fine cocktail of excellent readings and a deep sense of despair, Alborghetti's curiosity and attention have focussed on another hell of daily life, mapped in Directory of the Vulnerable with a painful lucidity in all its meanders, its darker zones and its most unsavoury corners. The starting point is unusual – one of the numerous tragedies of recent years, accompanied by the media hype that we all know: a mother kills her son in a provincial village (a geographic village but also a psychic village or suburb: the place, perhaps, where we all live). Alborghetti tries to comprehend and, yet again, he chooses direct observation and personal exploration, not so much of the protagonists of the drama, who are unavailable (or describable only in the distorting mirrors of journalists' disinformation) but of the place which by way of allegory, contains and channels the tragedy: the supermarket with its vision of a commercialized existence, of goods on sale and being promoted, of examples of pre-packaged and paralysed lives. The real supermarket, the place (or non-place) par excellence for communal life, but also the virtual supermarket where news of scandals and media talk-shows diffuse and exaggerate to their limits. In following up one of his trails, the author follows the customers, and families in particular; he spies on their choices, their movements, records fragments of their dialogues, their likely dreams, their inevitable catastrophes: he does this within the concrete reality of the shop, and the streets of the city or the suburb, and also within the virtual reality of television and internet sites, via the cruel creation of spectacle that in recent decades has foraged hysterically in the sorrows of an Italian family, constantly drifting towards being wrecked, towards self-destruction, towards infanticide, and which the opening of Canto 38 pins down:

9

Canto 38

Quando accadono quei fatti ecco, appare la tivù
a riprendere la casa
con davanti chi commenta, il microfono alle labbra

come fosse una preghiera, sussurrare concitato gli sviluppi della cosa
poi la ridda di interviste per sapere di quei fatti
e il passante va fermato che ci dica un suo qualcosa

nella gloria nazionale, apparire in tre minuti
per spiegare almeno un fatto anche quello più privato
un aneddoto preciso

(When these facts happen, the TV turns up
to take shots of the house
with a commentator in front, a microphone at his lips

as it were a prayer, muttering excitedly of developments in the event
then the round of interviews to establish these facts
and the passer-by stopped so he could say something

in the national interest, to turn up for three minutes
to explain at least a fact no matter how private
a precise anecdote)

Such a group of themes – more than unusual for a collection of poetry – shows with how much attention and how much expectation one should approach Fabiano Alborghetti's new book, so different in comparison to more generalised (and often soporific) examples: here there is no talk of the self and its troubles, nor of subjective despairs; the narrator's voice conveys a pure gaze, a gesture of awareness and of responsiveness, no heightened emotion. And our interest is increased by the author's surprising expressive choices, as he builds his cantos (an unexpected term, which is not to be understood as simple irony: we are, it is true, far from the traditional "poetic song"; and yet, emanating from this brutalised and commercialised region, it remains a song which seems to be aimed at other people – without forgetting that cantos are, first and foremost,

Dante's…). His cantos have a basis of an octosyllabic line that is almost obsessive in its monotone, but that is broken by a verse sometimes suddenly cut off, sometimes drawn out in the plaint of a hypermeter, of an intentional rhythmic imperfection:

Canto 4

[…]
Occorre molto, occorre avere
per sapere che felici non si accade e il prodotto è un senso primo
colma fitto ogni altro smarrimento: è una vita che lavoro

e certe cose sono diritto come prendere il prodotto
senza il marcio della rogna senza essere fregati
e chi si fida di quei nomi, i mai sentiti alla tivù?

Poi la fame nominava: niente basta
mentre fuori nel parcheggio tra le auto tutte in fila
il carrello accanto e pieno

scaricava nel baule,
ogni sporta chiusa bene perché niente si smarrisse
perché nulla andasse perso

fosse preda d'altre mani…

[…]
(You need a lot, you need something
to know that you don't just get happy and goods matter
and fill the gaps: I've been working my whole life

and I've got a right to some things, such as buying something
without the grind of hassle, without being cheated
and why trust brands that you've never heard of on the TV?

Then he got on to cravings: there is never enough
while he was outside in the car park with all the cars lined-up
the cart full beside him

he would load into the boot,
every shopping bag properly closed so that nothing would get

11

     misplaced
nothing would get lost

or fall into the wrong hands...)

    This octosyllable – sometimes revealed sometimes concealed; often redoubled to form a long verse; always likely to re-emerge in a despairing monotone – is like a nostalgia that envelops and distances everything; like an unattainable desire which fills lives with dissatisfaction or rage. This effect is the most obvious: it produces an extended rhythmic background, softly sounding, a little like a tragic or grotesque chorus:

Canto 5

Metteva il figlio in fondo al dire con l'orgoglio
del buon seme messo bene nella donna e ne vantava in ampi gesti
con parole da rivista da barbiere: figlio forte

ripeteva quando cresce come me deve pensare
e poi gli insegno anche il mestiere. Lo prendeva per le spalle
lo scoteva come merce mentre il figlio gli annuiva

troppo intenso d'emozione per quel ruolo designato...

(He kept on talking about "my son," with pride in
good seed well planted in the woman, and with wide gestures
    he bragged about it
with words picked up from a magazine in the barber's: a strong son

he said again when he grows like me, he'll have to think
and then I will teach him the business. He took his son
    by the shoulders
and shook him like a sack while his son nodded

overcome with emotion at the future laid out for him...)

The overall result is a compact, coherent and troubling book: its two aspects happily opposing one another – the almost unfeeling, almost scientific X-ray picture of a real situation; and at the same time the almost compassionate, almost merciful employment of that same situation transformed into short rhythmic pieces – co-exists in these poems, simultaneously hurting and pitying. The hurt is not the offensive result of a mere, disdainful condemnation; the comfort is not the honeyed result of a too easy and painless forgiveness. Clarity and compassion temper and strengthen each other; the reader soaks up the voice and, indeed, the canto. But this is a voice that is incisive, a canto that questions: a voice and a canto that Fabiano Alborghetti sets out to explore in perilous and awful places, once more risking to get lost. But he has been able on the contrary to re-emerge and to bring back to the surface this Directory of the Vulnerable: as strange as it may seem, this is, in spite of everything, a gesture of hope, an act of love.

Fabio Pusterla

AUTHOR'S NOTE

This collection arose from an incident in 2006, in a provincial village; a mother killed her own son. In the following months, the dailies and the television news provided all the details. From the display of daily information one image kept recurring, an assembly of facts: a photo of the mother revealing a young face, blond hair, a velvet band round her neck, elegant dress and an outgoing provocative pose. An image drawn from a fashion magazine, a photo taken from her past when she was seeking success as a mannequin, a model, a glamour girl. Her son was killed because his birth ended this dream. This book was composed in a similar way to its predecessor, *The Opposite Bank* (*L'opposta riva*, 2006): by observing what was happening on the ground itself. For a long while I had in fact infiltrated myself into the different family groups, noting their behaviours, the dialogues, the different relations that govern the physical, oral and moral behaviour of a family. I followed them in the shopping centres, the boutiques, the restaurants, I spied on them among the stalls of a market or setting myself up behind the hedges of private gardens, listening and taking notes. A second and important source of information – as well as specialised writings – was stories from different sources, from reading dozens of different dailies to see how facts evolve and thus the speculations, rumours, the revelations of enquiries in the absence of concrete evidence, the din created by the vox populi when someone is arrested, the pricking of the journalistic balloon to the stage of silence when the story has gone cold and no longer interests people. And finally I have been able to detail the characters of my protagonists by observing people I have met and remembering the things I have experienced. I would like to thank everyone involved in this collection of facts and people.

Fabiano Alborghetti

TRANSLATOR'S NOTE

Fabiano Alborghetti's *Directory of the Vulnerable (Registro dei fragili*, Bellinzona: Edizioni Casagrande, 2009) is unusual in terms of style and content. With allusions to Dante and Pound, Alborghetti tells a story in 43 cantos. The almost hypnotic rhythm of these understated yet pressing texts lulls the reader into following an apparently uneventful account of ordinary lives and events. But at the heart of this exploration lies an unexpected and tragic incident. By showing the reactions of a credible cross-section of contemporary society, Alborghetti seeks not universality but to stand in the shoes of his subjects. Thus *Directory of the Vulnerable* is just that: a book about vulnerable human beings whose feelings and experiences are watched and recorded. What makes the book particularly interesting – and challenging to translate – is Alborghetti's use of rhythm: meters and cadences that contribute to conveying the modus operandi of the people in this story. I would like to thank Fabiano Alborghetti for his encouragement and contribution; and Bob Lowe, for his inspired and inspiring suggestions. I would also like to thank the editors of *La Libellua*, where earlier versions of cantos 1-10 were published (n. 4, 2012, pp. 123-135).

Marco Sonzogni

PICTURES AT AN EXHIBITION
QUADRI DI UN'ESPOSIZIONE

Chissà cosa vuol dire debolezza
forza, nella gente, spina dorsale.
Chissà cosa sanno quanti sanno
ciò che vogliono, che spingono avanti la certezza
di essere, come fossero da sempre
uomini, e per sempre.

Elio Pagliarani,
La ragazza Carla

È tutto fermo: una coda a mezz'aria,
un getto giallo d'urina, un ghiaccio teso
sui fotogrammi spezzati, un bambino
che salta e resta appeso
al suo gesto giocoso. C'è una casa
e del fumo e un paesaggio tagliato dal treno.
E quell'ombra.

Fabio Pusterla,
Ipotesi sui castori

Who knows what people mean when they
talk of weakness, strength, back bone.
Who knows what they know, the people who really know,
what they mean, the people who stress first of all the certainty
of being, as if they were around for ever
and would be for ever.

Elio Pagliarani,
The Girl Carla

Nothing moves: a half-cocked tail,
a yellow stream of urine, ice spread
on broken negatives, a child
who jumps and remains fixed
in his happy gesture. There's a house
and a river and a landscape divided by the train.
And that shadow.

Fabio Pusterla,
Hypotheses about Beavers

Canto 1

Gli bastavano i ritagli le riviste che comprava in settimana per
    sapere
della vita e certe foto conservava per copiarne il buon vestire
la postura che allo specchio ripeteva in precisione:

il tre quarti dello sguardo, il sorriso di chi vince la partita...

Canto 1

A week's worth of magazine clippings kept him up to date
with life and he saved some of the pictures so that he could choose
   his fine clothes
and the expressions he practised so precisely in the mirror:

the three-quarter pose, the champion's smile...

Canto 2

Occorre l'ordine al vestire, occorre la coerenza
per l'inganno. Cosi ripeteva mentre a mani lisce tutto il bordo
della giacca a risalire, i risvolti, la camicia intonsa attorno al collo

troppo stretta eppure esatta per l'immagine allo specchio.
Un ampio gesto, un ritocco anche ai capelli
già perfetti nell'assetto e tutto il resto: perfezione ripeteva

offrirsi certi come il volto di quell'uomo imparato alla tivù.
Sono meglio a ben vedere, anche più vero:
guardava gli occhi nel riflesso, l'adesione

dell'immagine per il verso che voleva...
Anche la pelle era esatta nel colore, con il tono preso a tempo
nel solarium dietro casa. Perfezione ripeteva

e si mostrava sulla porta alla moglie già vestita.
Mano a mano senza dire. Non dicevano mai nulla. Troppo spesso
non trovavano che dire. E non trovava altre cose a ben vedere:

una ragione per restare soprattutto...

Canto 2

Clothes require order, illusion needs coherence
he repeated this as he ran his hands lightly over the cut
of his jacket, its sleeves, his crisp white collar

too tight but it looked just right in the mirror.
A broad gesture, a slight ruffle to his perfect hair,
and all the rest. Perfection, he said again.

Show yourself confidently like that cool guy on the TV.
Look carefully and I am better, even more sincere:
he watched the reflection of his eyes,

matching the image he wanted...
Even the colour of his skin was just right, the tan from sessions
at the solarium next door. Perfection, he said again

and at the door he showed himself off to his wife who was already
    dressed.
Hand in hand without a word. They never said anything. Too
    often
they had nothing to talk about. And, come to think of it, he didn't
    have much to say:

above all, a reason to stay...

Canto 3

Poi la sera c'era il film, da guardare sul divano tutti fermi
c'era il film e se piace ne facciamo un duplicato.
Mi conviene noleggiare e magari li rivendo ai colleghi giù in
    ufficio

cinque franchi ad ogni copia: è cosi che si guadagna
e annuiva con il braccio attorno al figlio, con la mano sulla spalla
come a dire mi hai capito? che tuo padre sa gli affari

e annuiva di certezze che sapeva d'insegnare...

Canto 3

Then in the evening there was the film, to watch on the couch
    with everybody quiet
there was the film and if we like it we can make a copy
I prefer to rent and perhaps I can on-sell copies to the people at
    work

five bucks a copy: that's the way to make money
and he nodded, his arm round his son and a hand on his shoulder
as if to say do you get me? Your dad knows his business

and nodded certain of what he knew he could teach...

Canto 4

Occorrevano quei riti alla forma di famiglia
allo stato fermo e ricco di famiglia benestante:
il bambino da lasciare nel recinto a piano terra

con lo scivolo ed i giochi, con le bolle in gommapiuma
poi ognuno alla funzione, certi acquisti nel carrello
da riempire in ogni spazio, certe marche che sapeva

esser meglio come il detto chi più spende meno spende
e l'offerta raccoglieva, il tre per due con il regalo
con il punto che spedito mette in gara all'estrazione.

Occorre molto, occorre avere
per sapere che felici non si accade e il prodotto è un senso primo
colma fitto ogni altro smarrimento: è una vita che lavoro

e certe cose sono diritto come prendere il prodotto
senza il marcio della rogna senza essere fregati
e chi si fida di quei nomi, i mai sentiti alla tivù?

Poi la fame nominava: niente basta
mentre fuori nel parcheggio tra le auto tutte in fila
il carrello accanto e pieno

scaricava nel baule,
ogni sporta chiusa bene perché niente si smarrisse
perché nulla andasse perso

fosse preda d'altre mani...

Canto 4

Those rituals were needed for the decorum of the family,
for the proper running of a well-off family:
the child to be left in the enclosure on the ground floor

with the slide and the toys, with the foamrubber
then everyone off to their task, every corner of the trolley
to be filled with selected products, with the brands he knew

were better; as the saying goes, whoever spends more spends
    better
and he would take up the offers, get three for the price of two
    with the gift
and the points you mail to enter the draw.

You need a lot, you need something
to know that you don't just get happy and goods matter
and fill the gaps: I've been working my whole life

and I've got a right to some things, such as buying something
without the grind of hassle, without being cheated
and why trust brands that you've never heard of on TV?

Then he got on to cravings: there is never enough
while he was outside in the car park with all the cars lined-up
the cart full beside him

he would load into the boot,
every shopping bag properly closed so that nothing would get
    misplaced
nothing would get lost

or fall into the wrong hands...

Canto 5

Metteva il figlio in fondo al dire con l'orgoglio
del buon seme messo bene nella donna e ne vantava in ampi gesti
con parole da rivista da barbiere: figlio forte

ripeteva quando cresce come me deve pensare
e poi gli insegno anche il mestiere. Lo prendeva per le spalle
lo scoteva come merce mentre il figlio gli annuiva

troppo intenso d'emozione per quel ruolo designato...

Canto 5

He kept on talking about "my son," with pride in
good seed well planted in the woman, and with wide gestures he
    bragged about it
with words picked up from a magazine in the barber's: a strong
    son

he said again when he grows like me he'll have to think
and then I will teach him the business. He took his son by the
    shoulders
and shook him like a sack while his son nodded

overcome with emotion at the future laid out for him...

Canto 6

Ogni giorno a mezzogiorno accendeva la tivù
per guardare la puntata, quella soap di vita vera
ambientata in posti belli

dove ognuno è straordinario
nonostante l'accadere nonostante
i mille nodi della trama da seguire.

Parteggiava in devozione per la donna e i suoi problemi:
ricordavano la vita e non sembrava poi un copione
perché nella vita vera quelle cose per davvero...

E viveva quelle storie come un colpo al basso ventre
trapuntare le emozioni
nel trovare quel conforto

come odore di minestra quando scopre di star male...

Canto 6

Every day at midday she would turn on the TV
to the next episode of that real life soap
set in beautiful places

where everyone is exceptional
no matter what happens no matter
how intricate the plot.

She would feel deeply for the woman and her problems:
It was all so true to life and it didn't really seem to be made up
because in real life such things really...

And she would feel such a story like a kick in the stomach
warming her emotions
to find the same comfort

just like the smell of soup when first she's not feeling well...

Canto 7

Il collier con l'orecchino, col brillante da un carato
gli pareva un bel regalo, un valore dell'amore ripeteva
mentre in cassa il totale era battuto e pagava con la carta

come a dire che l'amore non ha prezzo né confini
e guardava la commessa coi capelli fatti a coda
ricercandole lo sguardo, sorridendo come a dire

le capisco certe cose, aspettando un suo segnale...

Canto 7

The necklace and the earring, with the one carat diamond
he thought was a nice gift, a token of love he repeated
while the till rang up the total and he paid with his card

as if to say that love has no price or limits
and he watched the saleswoman, her hair in a ponytail,
looking for a glance from her, his smile as if to say

some things I do understand, waiting for her to respond...

Canto 8

Se guardava troppo fissa la sua immagine allo specchio
scontornava la pupilla tutti i bordi e pure il centro, galleggiava
ad occhi fissi senza nulla da capire. Rimaneva nuda e ferma

rifrangendo nell'opposto, con le mani lungo i fianchi
risparmiando anche il respiro... se rientrasse ora qualcuno
se rientrasse mio marito sorprendendomi già nuda. Quel pensiero

nell'insieme era il filo cui aggrappare
contro il vuoto a centro pancia, contro un corpo inefficace.
Quanto tempo è già passato da una festa in cui elegante

sono entrata per ballare?

Canto 8

If she stared too long at the mirror
her eyes would distort every outline and even the centre, she'd
    float
staring, seeing nothing. She'd stay naked and still

in front of her reflection, her arms by her sides
holding her breath too... if someone came back now
if my husband came back and surprised me already naked. That
    thought

was one to hang on to
against the void in the middle of her belly, against her ineffectual
    body.
How long has it been since I made a striking entrance

to a party and danced?

Canto 9

Il discorso, la finzione del discorso per offrire la presenza
di buon padre buon marito che pagava in pizzeria:
poi girava con lo sguardo come fosse un po' per noia

stando attento a bilanciare tra l'attorno e la famiglia. La portata
di ogni sguardo, la portata in diagonale farsi largo tra la folla
per studiare soppesare nel passaggio l'ogni carne

tra i vestiti immaginare quanto seno o culo o forma
senza un niente tralasciato e sapeva che veniva lui veniva in ogni
   corpo
lo sapeva che ogni corpo gli piaceva come fosse ognuno il primo:

non il mio si ripeteva a bassa voce, non il mio di moglie accanto
non il mio di carne morta già mangiata consumata resa sterile dal
   parto
non il mio ma quello accanto

e non importa quanti anni, che vestito o peso o stile
non il mio ma la ragazza, non il mio ma l'ogni donna
l'universo di bastarde che si offrono per niente

io lo so, io l'ho capito, io capisco ogni finzione...
Poi il figlio lamentava
del calore della pizza della coca già finita

intrometteva un'altra volta. Portava un nuovo cambiamento...

Canto 9

What he said, the act he put on
as the good family man who paid the bill at the pizzeria:
then he changed his pose as if he was a bit bored

anxious to balance between inside and outside the family. The
     meaning
of each glance, the glance diagonally through the crowd
to study, to weigh up each passing piece of flesh

to imagine beneath the clothes, the breasts and the buttocks and
     the figure,
leaving nothing out, and she knew how he came, how he came in
     each body
and she knew that each body pleased him as if it were the first
     time:

but not mine, she kept saying, quietly, not me, his dogsbody wife,
not my body deadened and already consumed and made sterile by
     child bearing
not mine, but that one there

and it doesn't matter about clothes or shape or style
not mine, but that girl's, not mine but every woman's
from the world of bitches who give themselves for nothing.

I know it, I've got it, I understand every one of his tricks...
Then the child whined
about how his pizza was too hot and his coke was empty

yet again he interrupted. Once again he changed...

Canto 10

Sognava il volo e un altro corpo e non diceva
quanto sforzo per trovare
quella forma da velina cui sapeva appartenere.

Molto prima di sposare era diverso
ma il parto lei capisce, è il parto che rovina.
Dallo step lo sguardo attorno rivolgeva per trovare

un solo sguardo che posasse su quel culo faticato, fatto magro
sulla dieta che diceva la tivù. Poi a casa un'altra dieta
cose bio per costruire più che il corpo quell'idea:

l'organismo era diverso molto prima di sposare
altro il corpo fatto meglio per l'età.
Niente intralci o imperfezioni

non contava neanche gli occhi che fermavano un suo sguardo
ripassare tra le forme sode e ferme
che scopriva poco a poco e di cui andava fiera:

ogni abito perfetto e scopriva l'ombelico, ribassava
una spallina o le gambe accavallava senza pena o smagliature.
Guarda ora che disastro:

non più donna di un qualunque corpo sfatto
che vedeva giù al mercato. Non è questo il mio destino
ripeteva, meritavo altro destino

Canto 10

She dreamed she was flying, in a new body, and said nothing
about the effort to develop
the top model shape that she now knew to be hers.

Long before she was married, it was different
but you know about having children, children wreck you.
Doing step at the gym, she checked to see if anyone

was looking at her weary back-side, slimmer these days
thanks to the diet on the TV. And then, back home,
the bio diet to build up this idea more than her body;

her body worked quite differently before she got married
and her figure was a lot better at that age.
Effortless and perfect

she had relished the way heads turned to take in
her firm well-defined shape
that she developed little by little and of which she was so proud:

perfectly dressed, bare midriff, a shoulder strap loose,
and she could cross her legs easily and without a blemish.
Just look at the disaster she is now:

not yet one of those sagging women
that she saw in the market. That's not for me,
she said again, I deserved a different fate

che un marito sempre assente ed un figlio che risucchia
ogni stilla e paragone... Continuava sullo step
insistendo il moto fermo, gli occhi chiusi nel pensare

che all'uscita se un incontro... Le varianti immaginava
senza figlio o sposalizio ma un qualcuno farsi avanti
per offrire la rivalsa, dare un senso alla fatica

ritornare in superficie coi polmoni doloranti...

to having a husband that is never there and a son who destroys
all my style and vivacity. She kept up her gym exercise
with a firm step, her eyes closed thinking

about a romantic encounter at the exit... she daydreamed about
    lives
with no son, with no marriage but with someone who turned up
to offer a chance to get her own back, to give a sense of direction
    to her effort

to get back to the surface, her lungs straining...

Canto 11

Si negava come un corpo da proteggere assoluto
si negava rifiutando che tu pensi solo a quello
si negava allontanando le sue mani appena giunte

a toccare i lembi estremi del vestito dei capelli
certe dita che posate gli sfioravano la schiena, s'appoggiavano
sui fianchi nella minima pressione di quel dire sottinteso.

Non toccare rispondeva lei scostando
pochi passi per alzare quel confine
si vedesse era assoluto, continuando le faccende

come niente fosse stato. Insistendo appena un poco
generava il cambiamento: risultava forte e fiera
ribatteva come l'uomo cerca solo quella cosa.

Ragionate con il cazzo
ribatteva come fosse il dire un morso
ribatteva con gli oggetti che sbatteva sul pianale

come fosse quel rumore la chiusura del discorso
come fosse quel rumore un principio di violenza
da frenare o altre cose rimanendo poi in silenzio

e restava in quel silenzio un messaggio mai espresso
allungava le distanze, li frenava ai due estremi:
sono mesi che noi niente le diceva a mezza voce

mentre lei voltava forte la schiena a dire questo è quanto...

Canto 11

She rejected him as if her body was holy, untouchable
she rejected him not accepting that you only think of that.
She rejected him by rejecting his hands reaching out

to touch the edge of her clothes the tips of her hair
fingers placed on her back,
lightly pressuring her thigh to convey his meaning.

Don't touch me she answered him, stepping back
a few steps to reinforce the boundary
so that her authority could be seen, keeping on with her
    housework

as if nothing had happened. His insisting a little bit brought on
a change; she became proud and strong
she reiterated that men think only of that.

You can only think with your prick
she repeated as if in saying she was biting
she repeated banging dishes down on the surface

as if this din signalled the end of the discussion
as if this din signalled the start of violence
to brake or other things, keeping silent

and still, in that silence there was a wordless message
that widened their separation, that fixed them apart:
it's been months since we did anything he half-said to her

while she turned her back on him to say that's that...

Canto 12

Sulla spiaggia col costume con le forme in evidenza
il colore della pelle e la pelle tutta tesa si piaceva, era bella
come prima di sposare, sono bella ripeteva

e lo dice anche l'amica mentre insieme all'estetista:
quelle foto da sfogliare ripetevano la forma, rimandavano la prova
ch'era bella da morire e certi segni non vedeva

non i fianchi un po' pesanti maturati in gravidanza, non la faccia
tutta tesa di chi accumula stanchezza, non le mani
consumate dai lavori dai bucati

era bella e si piaceva, si piaceva
ma lontana non presente in questo tempo
dove tutto ti rapina, dove il tempo è sottomesso

alle cose della casa. Là in albergo
era vita da signora: con la cena preparata con la stanza fatta bene
la piscina con le sdraio con il bar e l'ombrellone

col servizio di qualcuno che ti serve in ogni cosa
basta solo domandare e si esaudisce il desiderio.
Riponeva poi le foto nel cassetto del salotto

ritornava in questo mondo dove niente è come pare...

Canto 12

On the beach with a swimsuit to show off her figure,
her tan and her taut skin, she was pleased with herself, she was
    beautiful
before her marriage, I am beautiful she said again to herself,

and her girl friend says so too while they are at the beautician's
    together:
a series of photos confirmed how her figure used to be, repeated
    the proof
that she used to be drop-dead gorgeous but she hadn't noticed

the way her thighs sagged a bit after pregnancy,
or how her face was lined by weariness, or how her hands
were spoiled by housework and washing

she was beautiful and loved the way she looked, loved it,
but far away not here not now
where everything falls apart, where time

goes in housework. Back there at the hotel
that was the life of a lady; dining à la carte, and the room service
the pool with the deck chairs the bar and the sunshades

with someone at your service for anything
you only have to ask and there it is.
Then she put the photos back in the drawer

she came back to this world where nothing is the way it seems...

Canto 13

Divagava con lo sguardo nel mimare l'attenzione
le domeniche di fede, il vestito tra gli scranni
moglie e figlio giusto accanto

se devoti o ammaestrati non sapeva. Interrogando
il volto in croce interrogava il come il quando
e se qualcosa per preghiera gli venisse ritornato

e quanti occhi può contare chi dall'alto vede e veglia
e vede tutti per davvero? C'è premura di salvezza offerta in cielo?
Questa è vita da canile sussurrava non sentito:

siamo in mano alla pietà, ringraziamo dei frammenti
che pensiamo siano ascolto. Cosa resta della fame non saziata?
Imparare a comportare è la questione:

nel bisogno ognuno un credo, un estrarre un amuleto
che risveglia a giorni alterni un potere d'intervento.
Son diverso ripeteva a bassa voce, son diverso

e guardava gli esegeti di quel Cristo appeso in croce
reso quota per martirio: si chiedeva e se non basta?
Basta credere nell'uno si diceva calcolando

o più efficace l'occasione, tutto il caso degli opposti?

Canto 13

He let his gaze wander while seeming attentive
on those Sundays of worship, the best clothes in the pews
his wife and son right beside him

uncaring if they were pious or well brought-up. Questioning
the face on the crucifix, he asked when and how
he asked if prayer did anything in return

and how many eyes could he count, he watching awake from up
    there
and did he really see them all? And did he care about salvation
    offered in heaven?
It's a dog's life he muttered under his breath:

we depend on piety, we are grateful for any crumbs
that we believe have been heard. What about our insatiable
    hunger?
You have to learn how to behave:

when in need, each has his own credo, pulls out an amulet
which invokes half of the time some power of intervention.
I am different he repeated in an undertone, I am different

and he looked at the worshippers of that Christ up there on the
    cross
torn by martyrdom: he asked himself, what if that is not enough?
Is it enough to believe in a universal being he said calculating

or to believe in chance, the whole debate about opposites?

Canto 14

Poi il figlio s'era perso, d'improvviso nella piazza
tra la gente nasce il vuoto dove prima stava in piedi:
e nessuno che sapesse, mai nessuno che abbia visto

la maglietta a righe viola, il cappello rosso in testa.
Che ne sai dello spavento gli gridava in pieno viso
che ne sai di quel dolore di una madre resa monca

che ne sai gli ripeteva delle ipotesi più infami
con le mani sulle spalle come merce lo scoteva.
Che ne sai delle rinunce

del dolore che nel parto ti divarica la fede
che ne sai del corpo a corpo che nei mesi si fa spazio
per lo spazio che reclami, che ne sai

che non sai niente: della vita come cambia e del tempo
che smarrisce
si restringe per sparire e sparendo ti risucchia

si travasa in ogni anno che ti vede diventare.
Che ne sai che non sei niente
la mia vita che frantuma genuflettere ogni giorno

quella vita che depredi perché tu ne sei presenza...
Tu non sai della fatica che comporta il proseguire
tu non sai che per averti ho rinunciato a tutto il resto

Canto 14

Then their son got lost, right in the the square
where he had been standing in the crowd, there was a space
and nobody knew, nobody seemed to have seen

the t-shirt with purple stripes, the red hat on his head.
What do you understand about this fright she yelled in his face
what do you know of a mother's pain, like an arm torn off

what do you know, she said to him again, about the most horrible
    thoughts
taking him by the shoulders, shaking him like a rag.
What do you know about the sacrifices

about the pain of giving birth, that tears your soul out
what do you know about touching you over months
and the space you take up, what can you know

you who know nothing; of how life changes and time
drifts away
and shrinks to nothing and as it disappears sucks you down

runs into each year that sees you changing.
What do you know you are a nothing
my life brings me to my knees every day

this life that you wreck just because you are here...
You don't know how much effort it takes me to keep going
you don't know that to have you, I have given up everything else

e rientriamo ora è meglio
tieni stretta la mia mano che ti guido fino a casa.
Proseguiva poi più calma: ogni madre è la memoria

di quel Cristo che si dice, ma nel fatto è quella madre
che nell'ombra resta e muore
che patisce la scomparsa

ferma ai piedi di ogni monte...

and now let's go home that's better
hold my hand tight and I will take you home.
Then she carried on, more calmly: every mother recalls

the Christ people talk about, but in fact it is that mother
who stays in the shadow and dies
who suffers the death of her child

unmoving at the foot of every hill...

Canto 15

Qualcosa spetta ripeteva, ancora poco e son felice: ma la donna
a cavalcioni nello sforzo non vedeva, né le mani né quei seni
sobbalzare sotto i colpi. Solo lei che le pupille verso il viso
    rimandava

un solo sguardo gli chiedeva che donasse almeno un senso allo
    sforzo
della carne. Fotti come un animale gli diceva a voce bassa poi
    veniva
con guaiti aggrappando alle lenzuola. A che pensi domandava
    appena dopo:

domani parto con mia moglie rispondeva, resto fuori
    nel week end...

Canto 15

Wait a moment, he said again, a bit more, and I'm happy: but
   busy as he was he couldn't see
the woman he was astride, neither her hands nor the way her
   breasts
bounced with his heaving. Only she, her pupils watching his face

beseeching him with a look to give some sense to the moment.
You screw like an animal, she muttered to him and then she came
groaning and pulling at the sheets. Just after, she asked him: What
   are you thinking about?

To-morrow I am going off with my wife, he answered. I'll be away
   for the weekend.

Canto 16

Non conosco il tradimento ripeteva con l'affanno, aggrappando
giusto al bordo per trovare l'equilibrio le parole
misurate con pacata dedizione:

questo è il tempo alla famiglia
poi le mani giunte avanti, gli occhi fissi dentro gli occhi
ripeteva le parole, gli diceva forme e frasi ed immagini evocava

anche indietro, già vissute: siamo uniti per la vita
credi forse che mi manchi un qualcosa che tu neghi? Credi forse
che ricerchi altri corpi o situazioni?

Credi forse che da uomo mi comporti da animale?
Io non so che altro dire
e mostrava sfinimento

quasi certo che convincere fosse un'arte non casuale.
Con chi credi abbia tradito?
Lei alzava ferma e dura e la schiena era un sollievo

poter volgere sul muro quel suo sguardo da perdente.
Ma che donna credi sia iniziava a bassa voce:
credi forse che non veda l'interesse ormai sfumato?

Tu non chiedi che il silenzio, tu non chiedi che del sonno
Io ti ascolto mentre torni, sento sempre
ogni tuo gesto: quel restare fermo ore a fissare la tivù

Canto 16

I've never cheated on you, he repeated with anguish, struggling
to find the right balance, to choose the right words
calmly, correctly:

this is family time
then the joining of hands, eyes looking into eyes
he said the words again, he came up with forms and phrases for
    her and recalled

images of the past that they had shared: we are a couple for life
do you think perhaps that I am lacking something you won't give
    me? Do you think perhaps
that I am looking for other bodies or situations?

Do you think perhaps that because I am a man, I behave like an
    animal?
I don't know what else to say
and he looked drained

as if strained by the certainty that trying to convince someone
    wasn't easy.
With whom do you think I betrayed you?
She stood up determined and unrelenting and it was a relief

to turn her back and keep her look of despair for the wall.
What sort of woman do you take me for she began in a low voice:
do you think perhaps that I can't see your lack of interest?

You don't want to be with me, all you want to do is sleep.
I hear you when you come to bed, I hear
everything you do: the way you stay glued to the TV

quei canali sconci e impuri su cui fremi con le mani
su cui passi tutto il cazzo che ti spegne la ragione.
Credi forse che non senta, credi ancora che non veda

i tuoi segni sul tappeto, quella sborra che ti spremi
quando fissi quello schermo, quando vieni in altre donne
io lo so che non ci sono

quando vieni e sporchi tutto, tu non chiami la mia bocca
per quei sogni da scopare, tanto basta la tivù:
gode meglio che tua moglie, non è vero?

Quante femmine hai sognato mentre in piedi il cazzo in mano
quante femmine hai lasciato per tornare con me a letto?
Meglio un corpo da vedere che cercarmi anche per sbaglio

meglio credere che fotti ogni notte le veline.
E di me cosa rimane? Donna tronca di ogni sesso, io che ascolto
il cazzo amato preferire l'illusione... Odio ciò che siamo adesso

gli diceva troppo calma mentre usciva dalla stanza...

your hands quivering over dirty filthy channels,
as you void your balls and your brains.
Do you think perhaps that I can't hear, that I can't see

the stains on the carpet, the semen you squirt
when you watch that screen, when you come in other women
I know that it's not me there

when you come and foul everything, you don't need my mouth
for these wet dreams, all you need is the TV:
it screws better than your wife, eh?

How many girls have you dreamed about with your prick in your
      hand
how many girls have you left behind to come back to bed with
      me?
Better watching a body than finding me even by mistake

better kidding yourself that you are screwing these bimbos every
      night.
And what's in it for me? A woman denied all sex, and I have to
      listen
to my choice prick's preference for illusion... I hate the way we are
      today

she told him too calmly as she left the room...

Canto 17

Stare attenti ad ogni gesto
cancellare la memoria al cellulare
era questo che premeva poco prima di rientrare

poco prima di rimettere le chiavi nel portone
risalire per le scale
ritornare col sorriso alla recita serale

con la cena, le notizie delle otto da seguire alla tivù
con i piatti già riempiti e mezza cena da finire
ritornare col sorriso, un accenno per un gesto

che veniva rifiutato... Si cenava con il film
gli occhi alti per lo schermo che aiutava a superare
almeno il tempo del contatto

delle forme messe accanto
a cibarsi d'altra forma, d'alimento e niente altro.
Lava i denti del bambino gli diceva a denti stretti

che sia a letto per le nove...

Canto 17

Be careful with every gesture
clear the mobile phone's memory
that's the most important before going in

just before inserting the keys in the front door
climbing the stairs
putting on the smile for the evening act

with dinner, the eight o'clock news to come on the TV
the plates filled already and the meal half over
returning with a smile, a hint of a gesture

rejected at once... They ate through the film
eyes looking up at the screen which did help
overcome the time in contact

of shapes side by side
eating another shape, food and nothing else.
Brush the child's teeth she said to him through clenched teeth

he must be in bed by nine o'clock...

Canto 18

Altre sere era diverso, accadeva che il silenzio fosse rotto
dalle grida, dalle cose manovrate come fossero appendice
e si rompeva quel qualcosa

si rompevano i bicchieri mentre altro proveniva
dal livore che dell'odio era adiacente
che dell'odio aveva forma

come il fiato che si espelle dentro l'aria di dicembre
e altro fiato appena dopo
mentre il bimbo non dormiva, ad occhi fissi rimaneva

con l'ascolto e la paura e non basta neanche l'orso
non bastavano i robot a difendere lo spazio: messi in circolo a
    vegliare
messi intorno alle lenzuola

non distanti dalle mani...

Canto 18

On other evenings it was different, it happened that the silence
    was broken
by cries, by a trail of things shifted around
and that something broke apart

that the glasses smashed while something else rose
out of resentment bordering on hatred
and which was like hate

like the way you breathe out in the cold of December
and another breath just after
while the child couldn't sleep, and stayed, his eyes staring,

listening scared and his teddy bear wasn't enough,
and his robots weren't enough to protect his space; on guard set
    in a circle
set around his bed

just out of reach...

Canto 19

Poi la spesa si contava controllando lo scontrino, controllando
che un errore non venisse addebitato:
la cassiera ci sa fare, batte cose non comprate

e chi paga sono quelli che non hanno l'attenzione
io lo so, io te lo dico che poi passa a ritirare, mette in tasca
     l'eccedenza
passa in mezzo agli scaffali con la lista delle cose

torna a casa con le borse delle cose che ho pagato.
Lo scontrino controllava fermo fisso a lato cassa
ricontava ogni battuta, lo scontrino in ogni voce con un occhio

alla cassiera che sapeva menzognera.
La guardava di sottecchi con lo sguardo inquisitore, le diceva
a forza d'occhi io lo so che tu mi fotti e controllava anche due
     volte

poi finito se ne andava, appagato di giustizia che sapeva tutelare...

Canto 19

Next the bill for the shopping gets checked,
checked that nothing's been charged in error;
the check-out operator is up to it, ringing up items you haven't
    bought

people who don't pay attention, pay for it
I know all about it, I'm telling you she makes on the deal, she
    pockets the excess
she goes round the shelves with a list of things

she takes home bags of stuff that I've paid for.
He stands fixed checking the bill by the cash register
rechecking each item, every line with an eye

on the operator that he knew to be a cheat.
He watched out of the corner of his eye, he told
her by his expression I'm on to your conning me and he checked
    twice more

then finished at last he went off satisfied that justice had been
    done.

Canto 20

Certe volte giù al mercato con le mani messe in fila
innalzava il capo eletto, il vero affare che con l'euro si comprava
e non importa se il tessuto, non importa

se il colore è solo roba da cinesi
ciò che importa è che accostato altro stile posso fare: è firmato
si diceva ripetendo il nome oscuro all'etichetta

e comprava con la furia ne comprava ancora sette
di colori e tagli avversi che poi in casa li sistemo
si diceva ripetendo e domenica li indosso, la domenica al passeggio

dalla piazza lungo il corso
con gli occhiali da velina come ha visto alla tivù
con il panta con le trame che ricorda lo stilista e la borsa del natale

quella vera da mostrare con orgoglio e noncuranza. Tutto insieme
era perfetto era emblema di quel gusto che denota un certo stile
lei la moda l'ha imparata, lei la moda la conosce

Canto 20

Some times at the market, hand over hand,
she picked up the selected goods, the good stuff she bought with
    her Euros
and it doesn't matter if the fabric, it doesn't matter

if the colour is shoddy Chinese
what matters is that using it I can create a different style: it's got a
    brand name
she said to herself repeating the unknown name on the label

and she bought eagerly she bought seven versions
in different colours and sizes that I'll set out at home
she said to herself again and Sunday I'll wear them on the Sunday
    walk

from the square and going up the avenue
with the starlet's sunglasses like she had seen on TV
and her trousers with the exclusive pattern and a genuine designer
    shopping bag

one you could show off with nonchalance and pride. The whole
    ensemble
was perfect was the emblem of the taste which produced a certain
    style
she has learnt fashion, she knows fashion

e camminava con il figlio messo accanto, si fermava
alle vetrine si specchiava ammirandone il riflesso
e più perfetta del servizio da rivista che ha sbirciato al parrucchiere

si guardava mentre il figlio insofferente già tirava
per andare, proseguire o almeno camminare non restare
fermo al sole senza che la mamma guardi che son bravo ripeteva:

posso andare giù al campetto che m'aspettano, gli amici?

and she stepped out with her son by her, she paused
by shop windows and looked at her admiring self in the reflection
and even better than the magazine photo she had glanced at in the
    hairdresser's

she kept on looking while her impatient son pulled at her
to move on, to continue or at least to walk and not hang about
standing in the sun and mummy not noticing how good I've been
    and he asked again:

can I go to the football ground, my friends are waiting for me?

Canto 21

Gli diceva me ne vado
me ne fotto dell'ufficio, delle leggi del contratto, me ne vado
e ricomincio, me ne vado

e trovo altro, che il lavoro scorre a fiotti per chi ha mani e vuole
    fare
me ne vado e vaffanculo
e certi gesti poi mimava

come appendere il suo capo con un gancio alla mascella
come sbattere la porta ed uscire vincitore.
Gli durava una sera quell'uscita da ribelle, gli durava

appena il tempo di tornare giù in ufficio, ripassare a lato strada
riguardare la vetrina che mostrava quei cartelli
di lavoro interinale. Poi la sera raccontava che le cose stan
    cambiando

che si fotte dell'ufficio ma il mercato stà cambiando
e bisogna stare attenti
e bisogna avere l'occhio per cercare il giusto gancio, per trovare
    come entrare

che il momento poi gli arriva e lui sa la strategia
per lasciarli nella merda per andare quando è tempo e lasciarli nella
    merda
che non sai tu che vuol dire

Canto 21

He told her I've packed it in
I don't give a stuff for the office, for the terms of the contract,
    I've had it,
and I'm starting over, I packed it in

and, I'll find something else, work goes to the guy who can roll up
    his sleeves and get on with it
I've packed it in and fuck off
and he makes gestures

like hanging the boss out to dry
like slamming the door and leaving victorious.
This breaking out as a rebel lasts the space of an evening, takes
    him

barely the time to go back to the employment office, to walk
    down the street
looking at job adverts in the windows.
Then in the evening he would explain that things are changing,

that he may not give a stuff for office work but the market is
    changing
and you need to keep your wits about you
to keep your eye out for the right connections, to find your way in

that the time will come for him, and he knows how to plan
to leave 'em in the shit, to leave at the right time and to leave 'em
    in the shit
that you don't know what it means

e guardava dentro gli occhi della moglie che ascoltava
con la faccia da passiva, con la faccia del qualcuno che il lavoro l'ha
    lasciato
e non capisce ma si sforza di vedere quante astuzie

quelle esatte strategie che il marito va elencando
con la faccia di una madre che le cose ha rinunciato
con la faccia di chi ascolta cento volte le parole

e vorrebbe ritornare in quel mondo del lavoro
che alle spalle s'è lasciata per cercare d'esser madre
per fermarsi ad accudire

quella prole che per caso era arrivata
quella sera nell'albergo con la vista che del porto
gli riempiva tutti gli occhi

mentre con le gambe aperte il marito la riempiva
gli diceva le parole
e la riempiva forte e uomo e ci credeva in quel momento

e credeva che d'amore fosse pieno l'ogni tempo
e credeva che d'amore fosse pieno l'ogni gesto
che l'amore gli sarebbe poi bastato

per trovare quella vita, una vita che di donna fosse emblema
per trovarsi accudita
per trovarsi madre e forte con il figlio con la figlia

and he looked his wife in the eyes as she listened
her face unmoving, the face of someone who has given up work
and who doesn't understand but tries to see the dodges

the exact scheming that her husband is setting out
the face of a mother who has given up on things
the face of someone who has heard it all before

and would like to go back to the world of work
that she left behind to try to become a mother
to stop and to look after

a son conceived by chance
that evening in the hotel with the view over the harbour
that took her breath away

while, her legs spread wide, her husband stuffed her
and he said the words to her,
and he stuffed her good and strong and for the moment she
    believed it

and she believed that with love every moment was complete
and she believed that with love every act was complete
that love would be enough

for her to find a life, the life of a real woman,
to be fully committed,
to find herself a fulfilled mother with a son or a daughter

col qualcosa generato, quel qualcosa che valesse più la pena
del mestiere di modella, del mestiere di velina, che la forma poi
   svanisce
e cosa resta a fine vita? cosa resta della forma

di quel corpo in cui credeva se poi vuoto gli rimane
se inutile persiste
solo un corpo da mostrare solo un corpo

e niente altro, era quello il suo lavoro era quello il suo mestiere
esser corpo da vedere, esser forma da tivù
ed invece guarda ora, guarda me e la fortuna: esser madre

di rinunce, già sposata ed ho trent'anni
già sposata con un figlio, ecco
questo è il mio successo e non posso rinunciare, ecco

questo è il mio lavoro, e non posso licenziare...

with something begotten, something worth more effort
than the modelling business, than the trade of the bimbo, because
    your slim shape will vanish
and in the end what's left in life? what's left of your figure

of the body she believed in, if it just stayed empty for her
if it stayed unused,
nothing but a body for show, just a body

and nothing more, that was her job, that was her trade
to be a body on show, to be flesh on the TV
and instead, just look at her now, just look at me and my luck: to
    be a mother

who has given up, already married, and I'm thirty
already married with a son, what
a success I've had, and I can't quit, that's

my job and I can't resign...

Canto 22

Certe sere gli chiedeva di restare sul divano
perché russi e fai rumore e ho bisogno di dormire
vieni a letto solo dopo

vieni a letto quando dormo e fai piano nel venire
non svegliarmi perché dormo e lo sai che se non dormo
i mestieri van pesando, la giornata scorre male

e lo sai che io del sonno ho davvero un gran bisogno
e continuava con le cose, con un dire ch'era detto
cento volte in precedenza. Non sfiorava neanche il labbro

con il bacio del commiato, riparava per dormire
separata dalla porta. Lui restava sul divano
mentre lei s'addormentava, lui fissava quel confine

che non è soltanto un muro una porta tra le stanze
ma dell'altro, indefinito: stava fermo nel silenzio a contare
il suo respiro, a vedere quanto peso ogni fiato nello spazio.

Rare volte decideva di tornare verso il letto
a notte fonda stando attento, ritornare nel suo letto:
preferiva quell'assenza al dover partecipare, preferiva

stare solo nello spazio del divano. Gli sembrava una violenza
quel tornare a notte fonda
infilarsi nelle coltri

per dormire accanto a cosa?

Canto 22

Some evenings she asked him to sleep on the couch
because you snore and you are noisy and I need my sleep
you only come to bed afterwards

come to bed once I am asleep and don't make any noise
don't wake me up once I am asleep and you know that if I don't
    get my sleep
the housework gets me down, I have a rotten day

you know that I really need my sleep
and she went on and on like that, things said before
a hundred times in the past. She wouldn't even let her lips brush
    his cheek

by way of goodnight, she hid herself away to sleep
shut off by the door. He stayed on the couch
until she went to sleep. He stared at the border

which isn't only a wall a door between the rooms
but something else, unclear; he stayed unmoving silent counting
his breathing, weighing up each breath in the space.

Only rarely did he decide to go and lie down in the bed
in the middle of the night, carefully, to return to his bed:
he preferred to stay away rather than the obligation to take part,
    he preferred

to stay alone on the couch. It felt like an imposition
for him to come in the middle of the night
and slide under the blankets

to sleep by the side of what?

Canto 23

S'accorgeva della notte solo dopo molte ore
che a restare fermo in chat era un tempo parallelo e staccava
l'attenzione, riponeva i fogli sparsi con le mail di chi incontrato:

rimaneva in testa il nome
gattaverde o dolcemiele che dicevano le cose, gli mandavano le
    foto
con le mani attorno ai seni, gli mandavano i filmati che mimavano
    di bocca

mentre a lato sullo schermo la domanda lo incalzava
se ti piace cosa faccio
se vorresti di persona

e si toccavano in lentezza, gli mostravano la lingua
saettare dentro l'aria come fosse lui presente, gli mimavano
le cose e appariva il cellulare, quell'invito per l'incontro

che stampava e nascondeva
nei recessi del cassetto
che stampava e conservava

per sapere che volendo si poteva combinare...

Canto 23

He only emerged in the early hours after a long time
glued to the screen chatting, totally absorbed
he put away a few bits of paper with the emails from the people he
    met

some names stuck in his head
Pussy Cat and Honey Bun who told him things, sent him photos
with their hands cupping their breasts and videos where they
    mimed with their mouths

while on his side of the screen one question obsessed him
if you like what I do
if you want it for real

and they touched themselves slowly, they showed him their tongue
darting in the air as if he was there, they mimed
things and used their mobile phone, to text him to meet them

and he printed it off and hid away
at the back of the drawer
and he printed it off and kept

to remind himself that if he wanted he could fix it up...

Canto 24

Come gli altri anche loro certe volte se d'estate
il tempo regge, se d'estate con il sole: nel giardino la grigliata
con i tavoli le sedie con l'odore della carne

e il marito col grembiule con la birra che discute
mentre attorno coi vicini si ritorna sul lavoro, alle rate del pc
all'offerta che al super offre un nuovo dvd ma di quelli americani

e le mogli più discoste sotto il melo e dentro l'ombra
che si scambiano consigli tutte assorte dentro il ruolo
e a turno ognuna chiama con il nome il proprio figlio

che divincola nel prato a rincorrere il pallone
che lanciato contro il box fa tuonare la lamiera
manca poco che si mangia

poi a tavola per lungo con il vino quello buono
da provare nell'assenso di chi sa dove comprare
e le mogli in altre cose ed i figli

a metà pasto sono andati per giocare, sono intorno
già divisi per le cose da inventare, chi si arrampica sul melo
chi improvvisa la partita le magliette a far da porta

ed il sole va scendendo ch'è già ora di tornare. Solo dopo
la certezza che la vita è come un film, col giardino americano
con l'unione da famiglie come ha visto alla tivù e tutto torna a ben
     vedere

e non estingue in episodi...

Canto 24

As other people did sometimes in summer
if the weather was fine, a sunny summer: barbecues in the garden
with tables chairs and the smell of meat

and her husband in an apron with a beer chatting
with the neighbours about work, about the hire purchase of his
    computer
about the Blu-ray marked down at the mall, an American one

and the wives a little way off under the apple tree in the shade
swapping tips about their role
and each one in turn calling their child by name

who's running in the field after the ball
which hitting the fence bangs the sheet metal
it's not long until they eat

then everyone sits down at the table with a really good wine
to savour in approval of those who know where to buy it
and the wives talking about other things and the children

going off to play half way through the meal, already
squabbling about things to do, one climbs the apple tree
another sets up a game with t-shirts for goals

and the sun goes down and it's already time to go home. Just after
the conviction that life is like a film, with a designer pool and a
    landscaped BBQ
with the gathering of families like she'd seen on TV and
    everything is as it should be really

and doesn't end like the final episode on TV...

Canto 25

Il Natale era vicino il Natale già attestava
per le luci appese ovunque e i negozi aperti sempre
le vetrine colorate piene di suggerimenti

e ascoltava con dispetto i messaggi alla tivù
col liquore il panettone con la musica ad effetto evocare il
    sentimento
e parlava con le amiche ed ognuna è già rivolta

a creare l'atmosfera, a comprare da mangiare, la tovaglia coi decori
la candela profumata in regalo a chi non conta
e il riciclo degli oggetti conservati nei Natali

che si possono smaltire stando attenti a non copiare
che si possono donare col sorriso di chi ama
che si possono incartare se non sono rovinati

perché insomma tutto costa e se posso risparmiare...
E dicevano dei giorni delle ferie da smaltire
e dei viaggi programmati, certe mete nei paesi dove il caldo è
    naturale

cosi faccio anche il trentuno con i fuochi sulla spiaggia
e ritorno rilassata che quest'anno ho lavorato
che quest'anno non ti dico la fatica accumulata

Canto 25

Christmas was coming, Christmas was already there
with the lights strung up everywhere and the shops open all hours
with windows gaudy with offers

and she listened irritated to the ads on TV
with liquor, panettone, with catchy syrupy music
and she talked with her friends and each one was busy

creating an atmosphere, buying food, decorated serviettes,
the scented candles as a present for people who don't matter
and the recycling of items from previous Christmases

that you could get rid of without copying someone else
that you could give with a loving smile
that you could wrap up if they aren't too shoddy

because in the end, everything has a price and if I can save
    money...
And people talk about days of holidays to be fixed up
about trips booked, to places in warmer countries

I do the same for New Year's Eve with bonfires on the beach
and I come back relaxed because this year I worked so hard
I can't tell you how tired I am this year

e ripetono lo stress ed ognuna che annuisce e ripete
che lo stress ti consuma la pazienza e che appena arriva l'anno
va pensato meglio il tempo e l'ufficio se lo sogna

che quest'anno siamo muli, che quest'anno
diamo un taglio a quel fare straordinari, che nessuno dice grazie
e che stress anche il Natale con il rito del regalo, col pensiero

del da fare, con il pesce da comprare
perché è una tradizione
e quest'anno l'aragosta l'ho ordinata in pescheria

perché quella allo scaffale
dentro il centro commerciale
alla fine sa di niente e che è una volta l'anno,

si può anche esagerare...

and they repeat stress and each one agrees
how stress uses up your patience and as soon as the year starts
time needs to be scheduled better and at the office they can forget it

this year they won't make us drudge like mules, because this year
we won't do overtime, no one ever says thanks
and Christmas is stressful, too, with its rite of presents, with thinking

about what's got to be done, with the food to buy
as per tradition
and this year the lobster I ordered it at the fish shop

because the one on display
inside the shopping centre
in the end it didn't taste that good and it's only once a year,

you can really go overboard...

Canto 26

Con le ferie a fine anno ce ne andiamo su in montagna
e guardava i depliant con gli alberghi stagionali
con le offerte tutto incluso ma che resti qui vicino:

non ho voglia di guidare e le code in autostrada fanno perdere
    giornata
io ho voglia di sciare ripeteva come un mantra
e vagliava soluzioni confrontava tutti i prezzi e le foto a paragone

per trovare il vero affare, con il pass di risalita, l'open bar del
    dopocena
o l'offerta in beauty farm come lei insiste a dire
per avere i trattamenti i massaggi con le pietre, la piscina riscaldata

che il bambino può nuotare
e magari fanno un corso cosi evita la noia
e se ci sono altri bambini

lo possiamo anche lasciare...

Canto 26

We'll go up to the mountains for New Year
and he looked at the brochures for the winter sport resorts
with their all-in offers some good places close to home:

I really don't want to drive and you lose days in the motorway
    jams
I just want to ski he kept on saying like a mantra
and he weighed up the alternatives, considered all the prices and
    the photos

to find the best deal, with ski-lift passes, après ski drinks on the
    house
or the offer on the spa just as she keeps on saying
to get beauty treatments, hot stone massages, the heated
    swimming pool

where the kid can swim
perhaps take lessons so that he won't get bored
and if there are other children

we could even leave him...

Canto 27

Non facevano la festa, nessun bimbo s'invitava
a festeggiare il compleanno niente coca e salatini
né la torta coi regali niente giochi fino a tardi

con le grida nel salotto
che una buona educazione viene data dal controllo
e la casa non è un posto dove fare confusione.

Non sei tu che ripulisci gli diceva per spiegare
non sei tu che spendi i soldi non sei tu
che curi il gruppo quei bambini scalmanati

e sai dirmi che succede se qualcuno si fa male?
Non sei tu che li controlli dal mangiare come bestie
stando attento all'aranciata che fa fare congestione

non sei tu che a fine giorno deve dare spiegazione
se qualcuno si ferisce se qualcuno cade a terra
io non faccio l'infermiera

e se qualcuno si ferisce poi mi vanno a denunciare.
Non ho mai avuto feste e ti pare che ne soffra?
E' una cosa per la gente che non ha alcun valore

sono solo genitori incapaci di educare...

Canto 27

They never gave a party, never invited a child
to celebrate a birthday, no coke, no chips
no cake with presents or games till late

with screaming in the lounge
a good bringing up means self-control
and a home is no place for confusion.

It won't be you that cleans up, she told him to explain
it won't be you that spends the money, not you that
looks after this gang of over-excited kids

and do you know what happens if someone hurts themselves?
It won't be you that stops them stuffing themselves like beasts
keeps them from making themselves sick with orangeade

it won't be you at the end of the day that has to explain
if someone hurts themselves, if someone falls over
I'm not going act as nurse

and if someone gets hurt, then they are going to blame me.
I never had a party and did it do me any harm?
It's something for people with no standards

they're parents who aren't fit to bring up...

Canto 28

Il corpo in fiamme gli chiedeva soluzione, un qualcosa
che calmasse che alleviasse quel dolore, la carenza
senza fine del restare dentro il nulla

ferma al centro del salotto
a guardare le stagioni, attraverso le tendine
il cambiare della luce che spogliava il verde fuori

l'età dentro il corpo infame che moriva lentamente:
si sentiva il sangue in fiamme. C'è qualcosa
che va fatto e spostava la mobilia, sistemava le altre cose

come fosse quel daffare una vera soluzione. Ripuliva
con la forza di chi cerca d'annullare cancellare l'ogni traccia
come fosse il suo sentire quella polvere posata

quello sporco maledetto che incistisce l'interstizio
che accumula e ispessisce che diviene una cancrena
al pulito che ci vuole e spostava pure i giochi sparpagliati nel
    salotto

li gettava nella cesta
li chiudeva con la rabbia come fossero inadatti
li chiudeva cancellando la visione di quei cosi

che ammorbano lo sguardo come fossero invasione
dello spazio da rivista che vorrebbe casa sua
come fossero infezione nello spazio della vita

che vorrebbe solo sua...

Canto 28

Her burning body demanded solutions, something
which might calm, might soothe this pain, this endless
privation of staying inside nothing

standing in the middle of the lounge
watching the seasons between the curtains
the changing light that stripped the greenery outside

age died slowly in her despised body:
she felt her blood burning. Something
had to be done and she rearranged the furniture, sorted the rest

as if this task was a real solution. She cleaned up
with the vigour of a woman who sought to remove any trace
as if she felt like deposited dust

an accursed filth that festers in the crevices
where it builds up and grows and becomes gangrenous
in the cleanliness that is needed and she gathered up even the toys
    scattered round the lounge

she chucked them in a basket
shut them away in her rage as unfit
shut them away to banish the sight of this stuff

which defaced the look as an intrusion
into the magazine vision that she wanted her house to be
as if they were a disease in the space of life

the life where she wanted to be alone...

Canto 29

Alla visita alla scuola era chiesto un genitore
che parlasse all'insegnante
che capisse l'accadere: sa, suo figlio è intelligente

ma non applica il sapere, non si applica allo studio
a noi pare che un problema, a noi pare che suo figlio
possa avere confusione e chiedevano di casa

insistendo nei dettagli
e chiedevano se sempre rimanesse in quei silenzi
come accade qui alla scuola fermo al banco all'intervallo

non si muove e non gioca, non si alza per mangiare
resta fermo in quei silenzi come fosse handicappato
e ne risente il rendimento se non gioca coi bambini

ne risente tutto il fare che la scuola è comportare
che la scuola è l'occasione di mischiare le esperienze
ma non gioca coi bambini, lui rimane lì in silenzio

e nemmeno interrogato mostra segno d'interesse
resta fermo sguardo al muro e non muove neanche un dito
resta fermo nell'assenza e non sente neanche il voto

Canto 29

For the school interview they required a parent
who would talk to the teacher
who could read between the lines: you know, your child is smart

but he doesn't apply what he knows, he isn't committed to
    studying
to us there seems to be a problem, to us it seems that your child
might be confused and they ask about things at home

they insist on going into details
and they ask if he always stayed so silent
as he does here at school, keeping to his seat in the break

he doesn't move and he doesn't play, he doesn't get up to eat
he stays fixed in silence as if he was intellectually handicapped
and his progress is affected if he won't play with the other kids

everything is held up because schooling is about behaviour
because schooling is about different experiences
but he doesn't play with the other children, he stays there silent

and even when he is asked a question, he doesn't react
he stays not moving a finger, looking at the wall
he is vacant and doesn't even listen when his mark is read out

non risponde alle domande e resta fermo senza dire.
E chiedevano di casa se andava tutto bene, se in famiglia l'armonia
o se fosse un altro caso, se non fosse quel bimbo forse

un poco handicappato e in quel caso c'è il sostegno
per studiare le lezioni l'insegnante di sostegno
e suggeriamo di accettare

che il sostegno è un buon aiuto è un aiuto dedicato
per quei casi di bambini che dimostrano problemi
suggeriamo d'accettare per il bene del bambino

che son cose da pagare quando il bimbo cresce e lascia
che son cose e van corrette prima che sia troppo tardi
e per come van le cose non c'è altra soluzione

che il marchio handicappato in pagella è quasi certo
e chiudeva l'argomento per parlare con un altro
col dovere d'insegnante che ha capito un caso umano

e c'è un altro caso aperto a cui tendere la mano...

he doesn't answer questions and stays still saying nothing.
And they asked if everything was alright at home, if there was
    harmony
or if something else wrong, if this child was perhaps

slightly intellectually handicapped and if so, there was support
remedial teaching the remedial teacher
and we suggest acceptance

that remedial teaching is helpful, is useful
in cases where children are having problems
we suggest you accept for the good of the child

this kind of thing pays off when the child gets older and leaves
    school
this kind of thing needs to be fixed before it is too late
and given the situation there is no other solution

and the label of intellectually handicapped in the report is almost
    certain
and he closed off the discussion to talk to someone else
to do his job as a teacher who has coped with a human situation

and there is another case to deal with and he turns to greet the
    next...

Canto 30

Sei contento di venirci gli diceva fermo in cassa
con la coda della gente per salire sulla giostra
e le spalle gli teneva per non farlo allontanare

mentre attorno le attrazioni, tutti i suoni della fiera.
Non capisco la tua scelta gli chiedeva a mezza voce
il volere roba ferma mentre altro da provare:

guarda invece il tagadà o il vascello della morte
quelle sono cose vere non la smorfia dei cavalli
non la musica da donna

ma il brivido del vuoto. Indicava l'orizzonte
gli mostrava il thunderbird insistendo
che da uomo certe cose sono meglio

non le giostre da donnette e chiedeva
vuoi che andiamo?
Il bambino non diceva ma scoteva un po' la testa

ricordava l'anno addietro perché c'era già salito
e quel vuoto nella pancia quella forza che ti svuota
mentre tutto attorno cambia e non sai dove aggrappare

mentre il vuoto va aumentando e continua l'oscillare
mentre l'aria va mancando e iniziava a vomitare
e suo padre che gridava, lo portava ai gabinetti

per lavare la vergogna, rimpiangendo un figlio uomo...

Canto 30

You're sure you want this he said to him waiting stuck
in front of the ticket office in the queue to go on the ride
and he held on to his shoulders so that he couldn't get away

surrounded by all the attractions, all the sounds of the fair.
I don't understand your choice he asked guardedly
wanting something static when there is lots else you could try:

what about the Tagada or the Ship of Death
they're the real thing not the wishy-washy horses
not this girls' music

but the thrill of the void. He pointed around
showed him the Thunderbird insisting
that for real men some things are better

not girly rides and he asked
where do you want us to go?
The kid said nothing but shook his head slightly

he remembered the previous year because he had got on
and the hole wrenched in his stomach by the force
while everything spins and you can't hang on

while the hole keeps growing and keeps on and the swinging
    continues
shaking him and he couldn't breathe and he started to vomit
and his father shouted at him, took him to the toilets

to wash off the shame, longing for a he-man son...

Canto 31

Le rotelle aveva tolto dalla bici per andare
come i grandi gli diceva mentre il bimbo pedalava
col manubrio stretto forte, l'equilibrio traballante

di chi cerca d'andar dritto senza nulla cui appoggiare...

Canto 31

He had taken the training wheels off the bike to go
like big people he told him while the boy pedalled
holding tight to the handlebars, the shaky balance

of someone trying to keep straight with nothing to hang on to...

Canto 32

Nel lasciare la palestra col parcheggio già al completo
s'incontravano per caso, con quel caso ricercato di chi sa gli orari
giusti, ognuno con la borsa ai piedi e la pelle profumata

ognuno al massimo di forma nel sapere di sedurre
col sorriso da vincente ed il gesto ricercato
quel proporsi un po' casuale come fosse che davvero

quell'incontro solo un caso e parlavano per molto
ma di cose senza niente e ridevano di niente proprio come accade
   quando
ed ognuno è ancora teso a mostrare tutto il meglio

fino a quando un pomeriggio lui a porgere il biglietto
col telefono privato
a sorridere scherzando che in fondo non vuol dire

che se hai tempo in settimana ci possiamo risentire...

Canto 32

As she was leaving the gym, the car park already full
they met by chance, a chance helped by knowing the right
times, each with their sports bag and sweet-smelling skin

each in peak form for seduction
with a winner's smile and practiced gesture
slightly casual as if it were really

a chance meeting and they talked a lot
but about nothing and they laughed about nothing the way it
    happens when
each of them is trying hard to show their best side

until in the end one afternoon he gave her a note
with his private phone number
and a forced smile and a lame joke

that if you have the time during the week we could get together...

Canto 33

E se fosse che altrove o magari un tempo prima
e se fosse che altrove fosse data un'altra scelta e se fosse quanto
    fatto
un arrendersi alle cose?

Anche al prete la domanda
quando si era confessata
la domanda che tornava più frequente nei pensieri:

e se invece non sposavo?
e se avessi rimandato ad un tempo più corretto
cosa dice? e incalzava la risposta che sapeva già formata

che ammetteva ma di lato come fosse un poco infetta
un qualcosa da toccare con i guanti con il gesto
la distanza necessaria per restare immune sempre

per difendersi del tutto dall'effetto contagiante
incalzava la risposta per avere una conferma
domandava a fil di voce

e se fosse che ho sbagliato?

Canto 33

And what if it was somewhere else or maybe a bit earlier
or what if somewhere else another choice was available and what if
    all that was done
was just a way of giving in to things? of resigning to things? of
    accepting things?

She put the question also to the priest
when she went to confession
the question that kept coming to mind

and what if I wasn't married?
and what if I'd waited for a better time,
what would you say? and she ran after the answer she knew was
    coming

that she admitted reluctantly as if she had caught something
something to be handled with kid gloves with the gesture
the distance needed to stay always uninfected

to protect herself through and through from contamination
she chased the answer to get certainty
she asked in a strangled voice

and what if I got it wrong?

Canto 34

Abbassando poi la voce confessava i suoi peccati
come fosse una bestemmia gli diceva faccio i sogni:
è un qualcosa che risucchia

vedo i piedi dentro il suolo ma è diverso mi capisce?
Sogno spesso un camino che dal basso mostra il cielo
e una mole di persone con la faccia di mio figlio:

è mio figlio che ripete, è mio figlio
che moltiplica come fosse più una folla
e lo chiamo e lo respingo

e non so se faccio bene
e non so se miei gli ognuno
e risponde se lo chiamo, mi rispondono quei tutti

non capisco e mi confondo e resto ferma mentre piango
e si affolla quella gente contro il corpo e me lo schiaccia
mi spintona ed è mio figlio è mio figlio i tutti quanti

e gli chiedo ma perché hai fatto bua? Ma perché
non vieni a mamma vieni a mamma e lui avvicina
s'avvicinano quei tutti e mi stringono sul corpo

Canto 34

Then dropping her voice she confessed her sins
as if it were a blasphemy she told him I have dreams:
it was something that engulfed her

I see feet in the soil but it's different, do you see?
I dream often of a road that points from the depths up to the sky
and a crowd of people all with my son's face:

it's my son, each one of them, it's my son
and he multiplies himself as if he was really a crowd
and I call him and I push him away

and I don't know if I am doing right
and I don't know if each of them is mine
and he answers if I call him, they all answer me

I don't understand and I am confused and I stand crying
and these people press themselves against my body and they crush
    me
they shove me aside and it's my son it's my son all of them

and I ask him but why are you giving me hurties? But why
don't you come to mummy, come to mummy, and he comes
    closer
they all come closer and they clasp my body

fino a quando non respiro, fino a quando manca l'aria
e il camino ch'era in cima s'è richiuso e non dà l'aria
e non posso fare niente che restare tra quei corpi, tra mio figlio

che spintona che mi stringe e cerca un varco
e mi spingono in tremila, vanno avanti per passare
e trascinano anche l'aria e sono in mezzo e vado anch'io

senza altra alternativa, sono un corpo che confonde
sono un corpo dentro i corpi e quei tutti vanno avanti
e li chiamo col suo nome ma nessuno che risponde

mentre vanno avanti insieme e non so la direzione
perché intanto ho roteato perché sono messa dentro
e non posso che restare ed ognuno che mi spinge

e poi sveglio che respiro
come fossi ritornata dopo un tuffo senza fiato e sono sola
dentro il letto con accanto mio marito e respiro a pieno fiato

e sto bene in quel silenzio col respiro che ritorna...

until I can't breathe, until I am gasping for air
and the chimney up there is closed off and blocks off the air
and I can only stay fixed by these bodies, by my son

that shoves, that clutches me and pushes me aside
and there are three thousand of them to shove me, to go past me
and they stifle me and I am in their midst and I am carried along

with no other choice, I am a body in their midst
I am a body among these bodies and all of them are going forward
and I call them by his name but nobody answers

while they all go forward together and I don't know in which
    direction
because meanwhile I've turned round because I'm swallowed up
and I can only stay there and each of them pushes me

and then I wake up and I breathe
as if I had come up from a long dive underwater and I am alone
in the bed with my husband beside me and I breathe in great gasps

and in the silence I feel better now I can breathe again...

Canto 35

Occorreva l'attenzione e lo faceva già da mesi
ritagliare dei mattini per andare a far l'amore
lasciare indietro tutti i pesi per tornare in superficie

dopo avere salutato il marito sulla porta
dopo aver lasciato a scuola quell'intralcio di bambino
dopo essersi vestita come fanno le veline

gli stivali a mezza gamba ed il panta coi decori
con gli occhiali a tutta faccia come ha visto alla tivù.
Se non fosse la famiglia quella forma di prigione, se non fosse

la famiglia a tenermi incatenata e s'aggrappava
al corpo amante come fosse una salvezza
e faceva poi l'amore senza chiudere mai gli occhi

come fosse che col buio ogni cosa poi scompare...

Canto 35

One needed to be careful and she'd done that for months already
to cut back the mornings so as to go and make love
to cut free from her burdens to make it to the surface

after kissing her husband at the door
after shedding her hindrance of a son at the school
after dressing up like a glamour girl

the calf length boots and the patterned tights
the sun-glasses covering her face just like on TV.
If family life wasn't some kind of prison, if my family

didn't keep me chained up, she clung
to the body of her lover as if he was her saviour
and then she made love and never shut her eyes

as if in the dark everything might vanish...

Canto 36

Spiegazione era dovuta per quel livido sull'occhio
non normale si diceva nel bambino a quell'età.
Ripeteva la caduta, l'incidente per le scale

nel rientro al pomeriggio
ma il vicino le sentiva certe urla
e la madre qui negava: è bambino e poco attento

sfida gli angoli giocando.
Le braccia azzurre giù in piscina
si mischiavano con l'acqua

e nessuno le vedeva e nessuno ne parlava
che un bambino è poco attento
e l'estrema conseguenza è naturale

se palesa in altre forme...

Canto 36

Some explanation was needed for the black eye
it wasn't normal for a child of that age, so they said.
She kept on saying it was a fall, a trip on the stairs

coming home in the afternoon
but a neighbour heard some cries
and the mother denied everything: the child was careless

he was reckless playing round corners.
His blue arms in the pool
matched the water

and no one saw them and no one spoke about them
for a child is careless
and extreme consequences can be expected

if it happens in other ways...

Canto 37

Certe cose vanno fatte per trovare il giusto spazio
e serviva i piatti pronti ferma in mezzo alla cucina
con la luce innaturale della lampada a soffitto:

come fosse quella vita un qualcosa passeggero...

Canto 37

Some things have to be done to make enough room
and she got the plates ready and set in the middle of the kitchen
under the artificial light of the lamp in the ceiling

as if this life were something fleeting...

JUDICIAL THESES
TESI DEL GIUDIZIO

Chiamare qualcosa "causa"
è come indicare qualcuno
e dire: "lui è il colpevole"

Ludwig Wittgenstein,
Causa ed effetto

Ha il colore indefinibile del tufo
il geco che sul muro apre di scatto
le micidiali mandibole, azzanna
la malcapitata falena e non gioca
come il gatto col topo,
la tiene immobile in bocca
per un minuto che pare infinito,
poi scappa via tra ciuffi di sassifraghe
lontano quanto basta
per masticarla in pace, al riparo
dagli sguardi indiscreti.

Pietro De Marchi,
Replica

Calling something "the cause"
is like pointing
and saying: "He's to blame."

Ludwig Wittgenstein,
Cause and Effect

It has the inexpressible colour of tufa
the gecko on the wall snaps
its murderous jaws, bites on
the unlucky butterfly; it doesn't
play like the cat with a mouse,
but holds it unmoving in its mouth
for an endless minute,
then it disappears in the tussock
far enough away
to chew in peace, away from
tactless glances.

Pietro De Marchi,
Response

Canto 38

Quando accadono quei fatti ecco, appare la tivù
a riprendere la casa
con davanti chi commenta, il microfono alle labbra

come fosse una preghiera, sussurrare concitato gli sviluppi della
    cosa
poi la ridda di interviste per sapere di quei fatti
e il passante va fermato che ci dica un suo qualcosa

nella gloria nazionale, apparire in tre minuti
per spiegare almeno un fatto anche quello più privato
un aneddoto preciso

e si intervista dentro casa, perché mostra tutto e meglio
perché innato è il paragone con l'interno familiare
e non importa come o dove, se per strada o sul cancello

perché conta l'atmosfera per capire meglio il fatto
e non importa quanto fitto un contatto in confidenza
ogni fatto è buon mangime da gettare nella zuffa

anche il sacro fatto palta, anche un niente riportato
ed ognuno che arguisce superando gli inquirenti
ed ognuno costruisce ciò che afferma la versione

Canto 38

When these facts happen, the TV turns up
to take shots of the house
with a commentator in front, a microphone at his lips

as it were a prayer, muttering excitedly of developments in the
    event
then the round of interviews to establish these facts
and the passer-by stopped so he could say something

in the national interest, to turn up for three minutes
to explain at least a fact no matter how private
a precise anecdote

and they do the interviews inside the house, because that shows
    completely and clearly
because the comparison is innate with the family interior
and it doesn't matter how or where, if it was in the street or on
    the doorstep

because what counts is the atmosphere to better understand the
    fact
and it doesn't matter what the person interviewed knows
any fact is good enough to throw into the pot

e si trasmette lo speciale giusto all'ora della cena e ripetono
per sempre la domanda resa mantra: l'assassina
ha confessato? confrontando più risposte

gli elementi secondari non spiegati dal giornale...

even the sacred is dragged in the mud, even a mere nothing
    reported
and everyone draws conclusions far beyond those investigating
and everyone can colour their own version

and a special edition is transmitted at dinner-time and they keep
    on repeating
this question like a mantra: Has the murderess
confessed? Comparing more answers

the secondary elements unexplained in the newspaper...

Canto 39

Il commento a tutti i fatti si faceva col caffè
la mattina ognuno al bar per spiegare il suo movente
ognuno certo di sapere la perfetta situazione

e certe frasi colte monche ch'era matta quella là
e le madri di passaggio ognuna dire che vergogna
e il sapere il manicomio il posto giusto dove stare

e l'assassina va ammazzata
come dice la cassiera: che per me ci va il taglione
poi chiedeva a quel cronista

a che ora vado in onda che mi voglio registrare?

Canto 39

The discussion of all the facts happened over coffee
every morning in the bar to explain her motives
everyone sure of their knowledge of exactly what happened

and certain phrases picked up on the fly that woman she was a
    nutter
and the passing mothers each one said what a shame
and the right place for her was the asylum

and the murderess ought to be killed
that's what the cashier said; for me it's an eye for an eye
then she asked the reporter

what time is the broadcast as I'd like to tape myself?

Canto 40

Lo speciale era annunciato, il profondo più profondo
sviscerare l'antefatto, per trovare spiegazione nel dibattito col prete
l'analista, il sociologo scrittore far connubio delle tesi

così a cena o poco dopo ogni branco fianco a fianco
anche i figli parte in causa resi eletti e testimoni
ascoltare la condanna le attenuanti ben spiegate

di chi dice depressione di chi invece si confonde o preferisce dire
    altro
come ho visto il prete in nero che riprende il figlio in croce:
uno già era bastato che supplisse ad ogni umano

del demonio è la firma, la pazzia che va rinchiusa
e qui partono gli applausi per finire la puntata
poi domani altri interventi, il dissenso ben spiegato

poi gli appelli di chi contro di chi crede in altre tesi
ed ognuna è quella esatta
ed ognuna ha un suo passaggio, l'attenzione di un giornale.

Prende forma il sacrificio prima l'uno poi il suo doppio
prende ognuno ciò che serve, ti converte a colpi pieni
e non è una finzione lapidarne corpo o idea, farne croce bene
    appesa

Canto 40

The special edition had been announced, the background
was stirred up deeper and deeper, to find explanations in the
    debate with the priest
the analyst, the sociologist writer marrying all the theories

so that by dinner time or just after every group side by side
even the children got involved as judges and witnesses
to hear the condemnation and excuses neatly presented

by talking about depression or by getting confused or by changing
    the subject
like I saw the priest in black who talked about the son on the
    cross:
to take the place of each human being, one was enough

it's the mark of the devil, the madness to be repressed
and at this point the applause starts to finish the episode
then to-morrow other discussions, the opposing view well set out

then the calls from those against from those believing in other
    theories
and each one is precise
and each one is presented, is worth the attention of a newspaper.

The sacrifice takes first one form, then the other
each takes whatever is handy, convinces you willy-nilly
and it's no shame to beat a body or an idea to death, to create a
    well-hung cross

che ognuno si raduni nello sciame giusto ai piedi
e che ognuno almeno impugni della lancia il giusto estremo
e si bagni nel costato conservando l'espressione

di chi è giusto perché c'era
e il versante più sbagliato era l'altro e si vedeva. Noi che siamo
    verità
ripeteva un altro a lato, provvediamo alla giustizia:

siamo chiavi di un accesso che ad altri è negato...

so that everyone can get involved in the lynch-mob boots and all
and everyone can get stick their dagger in to the hilt
and wash in Christ's blood and water while maintaining an
    expression

of those who are right because they were there
and it was the other side who were misleading and it showed. We
    who are truth
another repeated aside, we are committed to justice:

we hold the key to something others can't access...

DIRECTORY OF THE VULNERABLE
(REGISTRO DEI FRAGILI)

Di quelle vaghe ombre
dei nomi cui corrispondevano
il tempo cancellava la memoria.
Come sassi lanciati sull'acqua
che affondano dopo breve corsa
le figure si allontanavano
svanivano nell'aria trasparente.

Giampiero Neri,
Armi e mestieri

Quell'ombra che mi segue per le strade
non toccatela, lasciate che si nasconda
ancora e ancora, sotto le gronde, si annidi
nei prati arruffati, si posi
dentro il carrello del supermercato
sui visi che balenano nella memoria,
che mi accompagni tra le tapparelle
e il buffet dove splendono intatte le stelle.

Alberto Nessi,
Il colore della malva

Time wipes out the memory
of these vague shadows
of the names they bear.
Like stones thrown in the water
that disappear after a few moments
faces move away
fade in the clear air.

Giampiero Neri,
Arms and trades

This shade that follows me through the streets
don't touch it, let it hide itself
again and again, under the gutters, find a nest
in the tangled fields, settle
in a super-market trolley
on the faces that pass in the memory,
let it bear me through the blinds
and the sideboard where the stars shine intact.

Alberto Nessi,
The Colour of the Mallow Flower

Canto 41

Non tra cose da città ma tra quiete da giardini
tra la quiete da famiglie coi parcheggi in ogni dove
con il centro commerciale

con il corso che è uno sputo dove andare a passeggiare
in provincia accade il fatto ed ognuno è testimone
prima o dopo ognuno ha visto ma nessuno nel durante

mai nessuno che sospetti che qualcosa va fermato.
È successo l'omicidio e questo scuote le famiglie
la coscienza più cristiana:

lo dicevano in paese che qualcosa non andava.
Sai qualcosa di diverso, chiede ognuno accanto assorto:
come accade che la madre uccida il figlio.

Cosa dice la tivù?

Canto 41

Not in the townscape but in the quiet gardens
in the quiet families with off-street parking
with the shopping centre

with the small avenue round the corner where you could stroll
in the country it happens and everyone is a witness
sooner or later everybody saw (something) but nobody at the time

no one ever thinks they have to stop something.
Murder happened and that shakes families
the most Christian of consciences:

people said in the village that something wasn't right.
Do you know something else, everybody there asks thoughtfully:
how a mother could end up killing her son.

What did they say on TV?

Canto 42

Ripassando accanto a casa non c'è niente da indicare
nessun segno della cosa che si possa ricordare
e tra casa e marciapiede quella siepe ben curata

che non dice grandi cose e sembra uguale alla vicina
che nemmeno sul giornale c'è più spazio o le parole
e se uno non sapesse, non potrebbe immaginare.

Hai la lista della spesa? dice uno da un giardino
e poco dopo la vettura, la famiglia che allontana
per percorrere la strada fino al centro commerciale.

Da lontano la villetta mostra segni consueti
con l'antenna parabolica che aspetta sul balcone
e il giardino con i nani e le piante giapponesi

e le sdraio ancora aperte, se ritorna un po' di sole…

Canto 42

When you went past the house there was nothing to show
no sign of the thing no reminder
and between the house and the pavement the neat hedge

which conveyed nothing and seemed the same as its neighbour
and even the newspaper didn't cover it any more
and if you didn't know about it, you couldn't have imagined it.

Have you got the shopping list? Someone asked in a garden
and shortly after the car: the family goes out
to make the trip to the shopping centre.

Seen from a distance the house looked ordinary
with its satellite dish set up on the balcony
and the garden with its gnomes and Japanese shrubs

the beach chairs still out, in case the sun should come back...

Canto 43

Lo vedevano passare ogni tanto nel paese
e si guardava quel normale che rimane alla tragedia
un mistero non spiegato da guardare con cautela

per ridire a forza d'occhi questo a noi non può accadere...

Canto 43

Every so often they saw him passing through the village
and they saw the normality that remains after the tragedy
an inexplicable mystery to be treated with caution

as if to convince themselves that sort of thing can't happen to
    people like us...